Water for Everyone

Ellen Lawrence

LIGHTBOX
openlightbox.com

LIGHTBOX

Go to **www.openlightbox.com** and enter this book's unique code.

ACCESS CODE

LBP94542

Lightbox is an all-inclusive digital solution for the teaching and learning of curriculum topics in an original, groundbreaking way. Lightbox is based on National Curriculum Standards.

OPTIMIZED FOR

- ✓ TABLETS
- ✓ WHITEBOARDS
- ✓ COMPUTERS
- ✓ AND MUCH MORE!

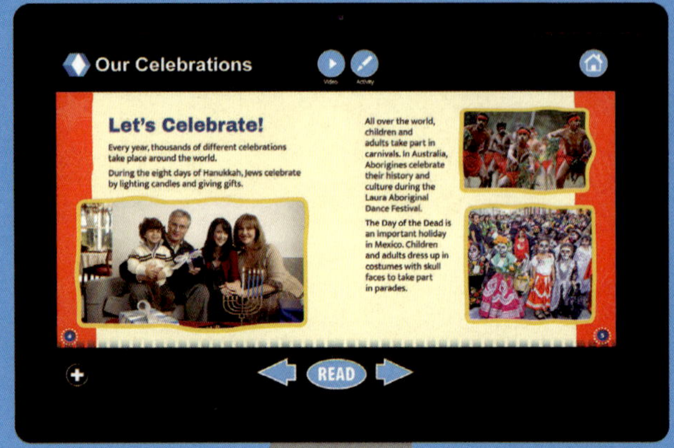

STANDARD FEATURES OF LIGHTBOX

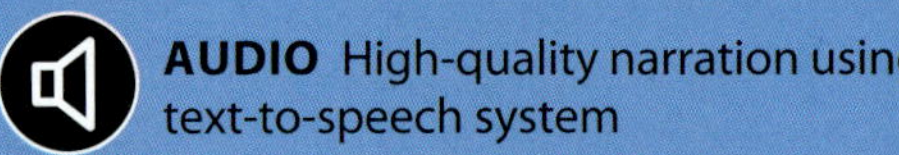

AUDIO High-quality narration using text-to-speech system

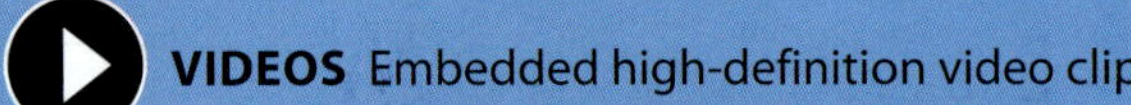

VIDEOS Embedded high-definition video clips

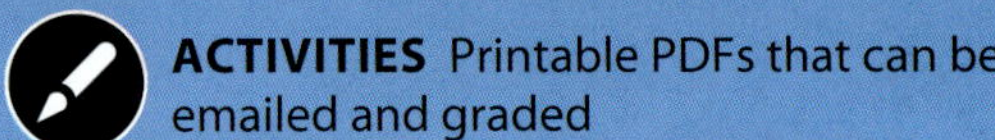

ACTIVITIES Printable PDFs that can be emailed and graded

WEBLINKS Curated links to external, child-safe resources

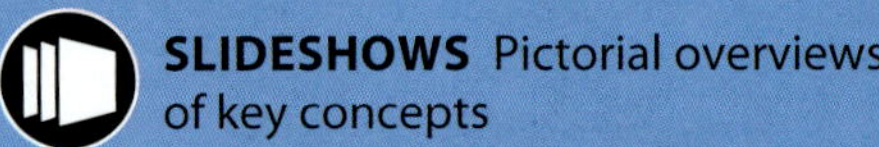

SLIDESHOWS Pictorial overviews of key concepts

INTERACTIVE MAPS Interactive maps and aerial satellite imagery

QUIZZES Ten multiple choice questions that are automatically graded and emailed for teacher assessment

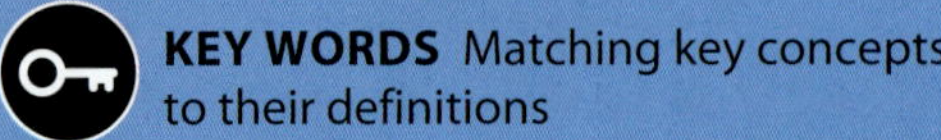

KEY WORDS Matching key concepts to their definitions

VIDEOS

WEBLINKS

SLIDESHOWS

QUIZZES

About Our World

Water for Everyone

Water in Our World

We need water to drink. We use water for cooking. We wash our clothes with water. We need water to keep clean.

We use water for keeping cool and having fun.

Water in a Desert

Humans cannot survive without having water to drink. Many people live in places where water is hard to find, however.

The San people live in the Kalahari Desert in Africa. The San know many ways to find water in this hot, dry land. One way is to drink rainwater that collects in small holes in trees.

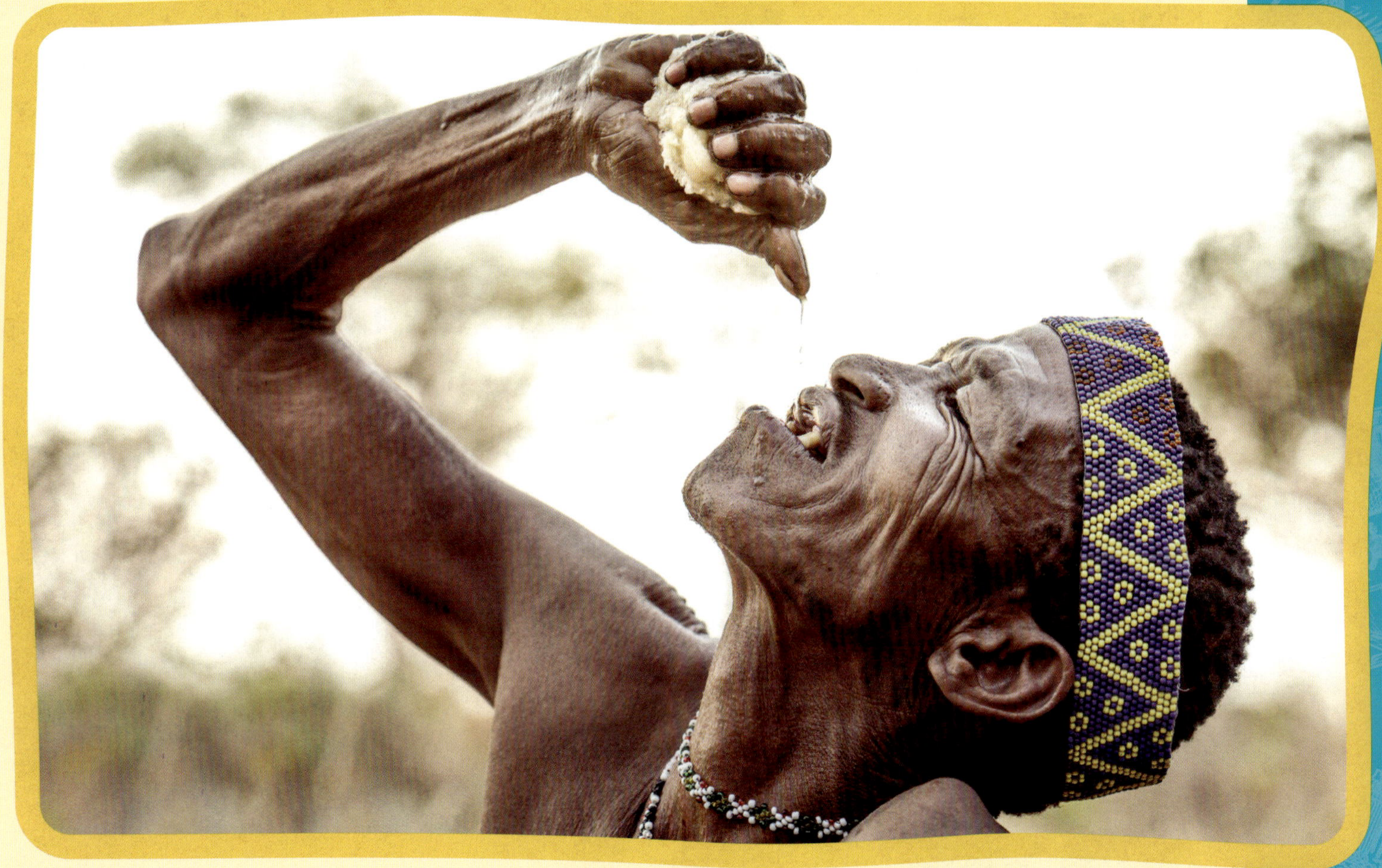

The San get water from the roots of plants that are known as milk plants. First, they dig up a root. Then they mush it up and squeeze water from it.

The red sands of the Kalahari Desert are more than 200 feet (61 meters) deep.

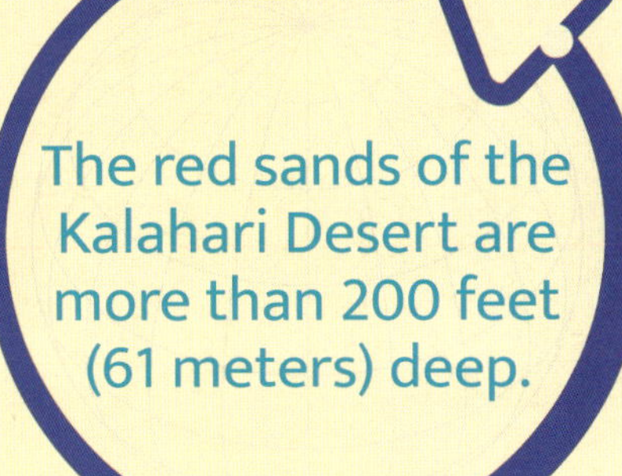

Water in a Frozen Land

The Nenets people live in Siberia in Russia. They are reindeer herders. They live in small camps and move from place to place with their animals.

The temperature where the Nenets people live is often much colder than inside a freezer. The water in lakes and rivers freezes into solid ice.

To get water, Nenets people collect snow. Then they melt the snow over fires and stoves to make water for drinking and cooking.

Doing the Laundry

Not everyone can clean their dirty clothes in a washing machine. Many people around the world do their laundry in rivers and streams.

To remove water from wet clothes, people hit them hard against rocks. The freshly washed clothes are hung outdoors to dry in the Sun.

Putting clothes in a dryer uses electricity. Drying clothes using sunshine and wind uses no electricity, so hanging laundry to dry is better for the planet.

No Clean Water

Millions of people around the world have no clean water. Many get their water from small, puddle-like waterholes, dirty streams, or polluted rivers. The water may contain insects and germs. Every day, thousands of people get sick from drinking dirty water.

In India, millions of people in cities have no water in their homes. Each day, people must wait for hours for trucks to bring them water. Often, the trucks bring only enough water for drinking and cooking and nothing to spare for washing.

Walking for Water

As the Sun rises each morning, many children around the world begin their chores. Their first job is to make a long walk to collect water for their families.

Some children have to walk for an hour or more to reach a waterhole, pond, or stream. Then they walk an hour back home carrying a heavy can of water. Many children have to make this journey three or four times each day!

In many families, it is the girls' job to collect water. The girls are busy all day collecting water and doing other chores, such as cooking. They have no time to go to school or play with their friends.

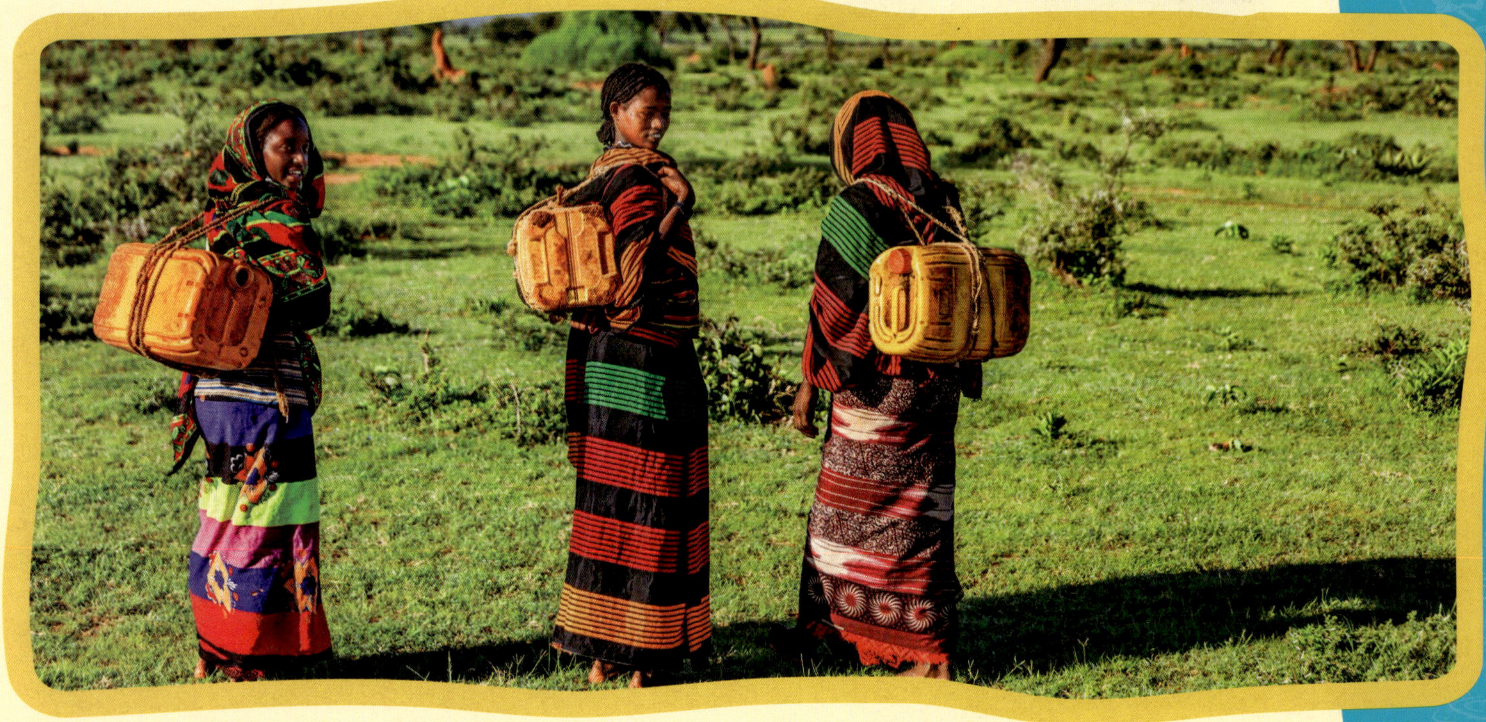

Digging a Well

In Africa, many people, especially children, spend hours each day getting water. They would not need to do this if their village had a well. It costs a lot of money to dig a well, however.

Sometimes, charities help poor villages raise money to build a well. Then engineers visit the village and choose a spot with water underground. They drill into the ground and put pipes down into the water.

Pipes carry water to a pump above the ground. When people push the handle of the pump up and down, clean, fresh water pours out!

Almost one out of every ten people is not able to get clean water.

Clean Water for Everyone

Once a village in Africa has a well, it can make a difference in all the villagers' lives.

Water that comes from deep underground is clean and free of germs. When people drink this water, they don't get sick.

Having plenty of water makes it easier to grow vegetables and other crops. Having clean water and better food makes everyone healthier.

If children don't have to spend hours collecting water, they have time to go to school. Kids who are healthy have lots of energy to study and play.

Turning Fog into Water

Some people live in places with little running water, but lots of fog. Fog is a cloud that touches the ground. It is made up of tiny drops of water.

To collect fog, people use a fog collector made of mesh, or net. The wind blows fog through the collector. The tiny drops of water in fog collect on the mesh.

The water from a fog collector runs into pipes and can be used for drinking, cooking, and washing.

How do people around the world get their water?

How does having clean water make life better?

KEY WORDS

Research has shown that as much as 65 percent of all written material published in English is made up of 300 words. These 300 words cannot be taught using pictures or learned by sounding them out. They must be recognized by sight. This book contains 120 common sight words to help young readers improve their reading fluency and comprehension. This book also teaches young readers several important content words, such as proper nouns. These words are paired with pictures to aid in learning and improve understanding.

Page	Sight Words First Appearance
4	for, in, keep, need, our, to, use, water, we, with, world
5	and
6	a, find, hard, is, know, land, live, many, one, people, places, small, that, the, this, trees, ways, where, without
7	are, as, feet, first, from, get, it, more, of, plants, than, then, they, up
8	animals, move, their
9	into, make, much, often, over, rivers
10	around, can, do, not, them
11	no, so
12	day, every, have, like, may, or
13	each, enough, homes, must, only
14	an, back, children, four, long, some, three, times
15	all, at, carry, girls, go, heads, on, other, play, school, such
16	had, if, well, would
17	above, almost, down, help, out, put, sometimes, when
18	comes, don't, has, once
19	food, grow, study, who
20	but, little, made, through
21	be, runs
22	how
23	does, life

Page	Content Words First Appearance
4	clothes
6	Africa, Kalahari Desert, land, rainwater, San
7	milk, roots, sands
8	camps, herders, Nenets, reindeer, Russia, Siberia
9	fires, freezer, ice, lakes, snow, stoves, temperature
10	laundry, outdoors, rocks, streams, Sun, washing machine
11	electricity, planet, sunshine, wind
12	germs, insects, waterholes
13	cities, India, trucks
14	chores, families, job, morning, pond
15	friends, heads
16	village, well
17	charities, engineers, ground, handle, pipes, underground
19	crops, energy, vegetables
20	cloud, drops, fog, mesh, net

Published by Smartbook Media Inc.
350 5th Avenue, 59th Floor New York, NY 10118
Website: www.openlightbox.com

Printed in the United States of America in Brainerd, Minnesota
1 2 3 4 5 6 7 8 9 0 22 21 20 19 18

012018
120117

Library of Congress Cataloging in Publication Control Number: 2017959800

ISBN 978-1-5105-3536-7 (hardcover)
ISBN 978-1-5105-3537-4 (multi-user eBook)

Project Coordinator: John Willis
Art Director: Terry Paulhus

Every reasonable effort has been made to trace ownership and to obtain permission to reprint copyright material. The publisher would be pleased to have any errors or omissions brought to its attention so that they may be corrected in subsequent printings.
The publisher acknowledges Getty Images and Alamy as its primary image suppliers for this title.